Art in
Action

Credits

Art in Action

Guy Hubbard

Indiana University

Contributing Educators:

D. Sydney Brown
Lee C. Hanson
Barbara Herberholz

 **CORONADO PUBLISHERS**

San Diego   Orlando   Dallas   Chicago

ACKNOWLEDGMENTS

For permission to reprint copyrighted material, grateful acknowledgment is made to the following:

BERTHA KLAUSNER INTERNATIONAL LITERARY AGENCY, INC: "Merry-Go-Round" by Dorothy Baruch from *I Like Machinery* by Dorothy Baruch.

MARIAN REINER FOR MYRA COHN LIVINGSTON: "Buildings" by Myra Cohn Livingston from *Whispers and Other Poems*, copyright © 1958 by Myra Cohn Livingston, and "Understanding" by Myra Cohn Livingston, from *The Moon and a Star and Other Poems* by Myra Cohn Livingston, copyright © 1965 by Myra Cohn Livingston.

RUSSELL & VOLKENING, INC: "Hello and Good-by" by Mary Ann Hoberman from *Hello And Good-by* by Mary Ann Hoberman, copyright © 1959 by Mary Ann Hoberman.

VIKING PENGUIN, INC.: Excerpt from *A House is a House for Me* by Mary Ann Hoberman, copyright © 1978 by Mary Ann Hoberman.

Printed in the United States of America   ISBN 0-15-770044-5(1)
  901 063 9876543

Table of Contents

Unit 1

Art All Around

What is **art**?

Where can you find it?

 Seeing Straight Lines

Looking and Thinking

Look at the **lines**.

Can you find straight lines?

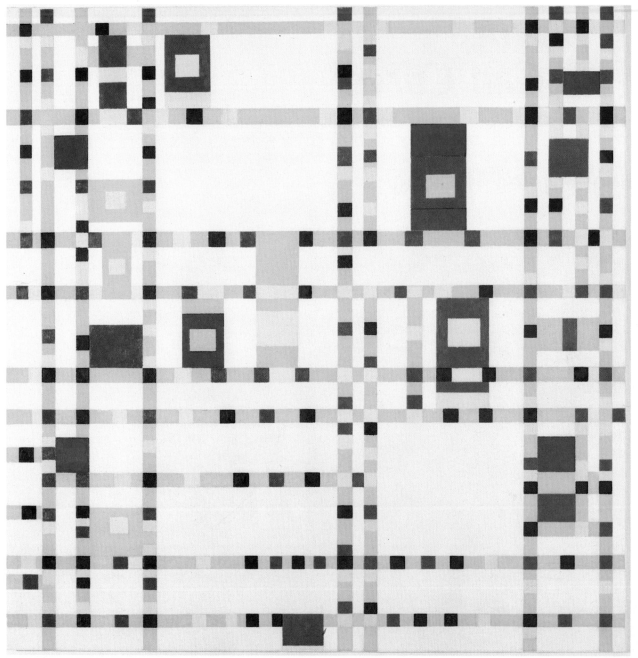

Piet Mondrian, Broadway Boogie Woogie, 1942–43, Oil on canvas, 50″ × 50″. Collection, The Museum of Modern Art, New York, Given anonymously.

The **artist** used lines.

What lines do you see?

2 Lines Can Curve

Looking and Thinking

Look at the lines.

Can you find curved lines?

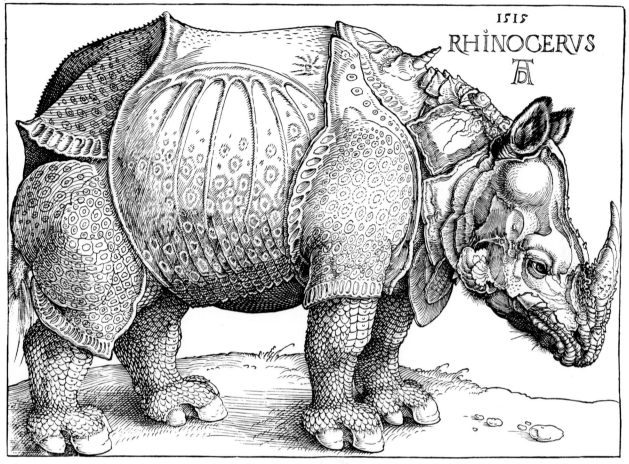

Albrecht Dürer, Rhinoceros, 1515, Woodcut, 8½" x 11¾". The New York Public Library, Lessing J. Rosenwald Collection.

An artist made this.

Did he use curved lines? Where?

3 Lines Show Motion

Looking and Thinking

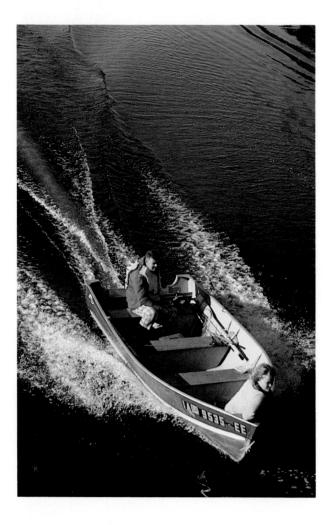

What do these lines tell us?

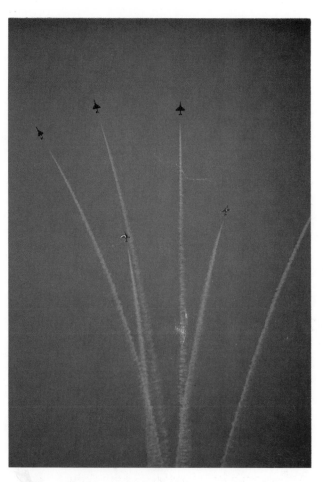

What do these lines tell us?

Where do these lines go?
What stories do these lines tell?

4 Lines Make Shapes

Looking and Thinking

les bêtes de la mer...
H. Matisse 50

This is a **collage**.
The artist liked to cut
paper **shapes**.

Which shapes have
curved lines?

Which shapes have
straight lines?

*Henri Matisse, Beasts of the Sea, [19]50, Paper on canvas
(collage), 116⅜" × 60⅝". National Gallery of Art,
Washington, Ailsa Mellon Bruce Fund.*

Juan Gris, The Chessboard, *1917, Oil on wood, 28⅜" × 39⅜". Collection of The Museum of Modern Art, New York.*

What shapes can you find?

Making Art THINK SAFETY

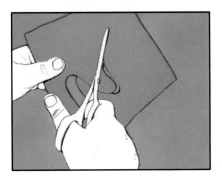

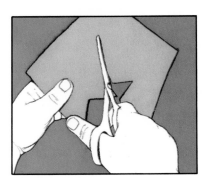

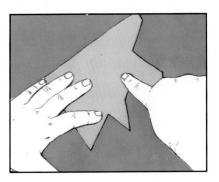

1. Cut curving lines.

2. Cut straight lines.

3. Paste the edges.

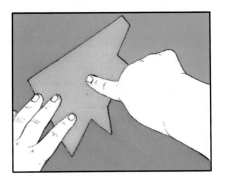

4. Paste the middle.

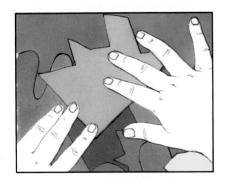

5. Clean your hands.

6. Press down.

5 Finding Shapes

Looking and Thinking

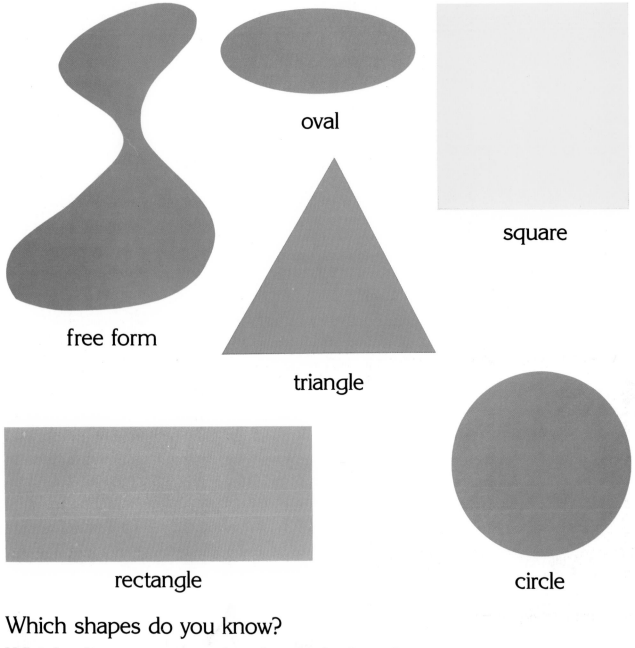

oval

square

free form

triangle

rectangle

circle

Which shapes do you know?
Which shapes are made of straight lines?
Which shapes are made of curved lines?

What shapes can you find in the pictures?
What shapes can you find in your room?

#
6 *Finding Shapes in Places*

Looking and Thinking

Where are these shapes in the picture?

triangle rectangle square circle

What other shapes can you find?

from
"Buildings"

Buildings are a great surprise,
Every one's a different size.
Offices
grow
long
and
high,
tall
enough
to
touch
the
sky.
Houses seem
more like a box,
made of glue
and building blocks.
Every time you look, you see
Buildings shaped quite differently.

Myra Cohn Livingston

This artist used shapes.
What shapes can you find?

7 *Finding Colors You Know*

Looking and Thinking

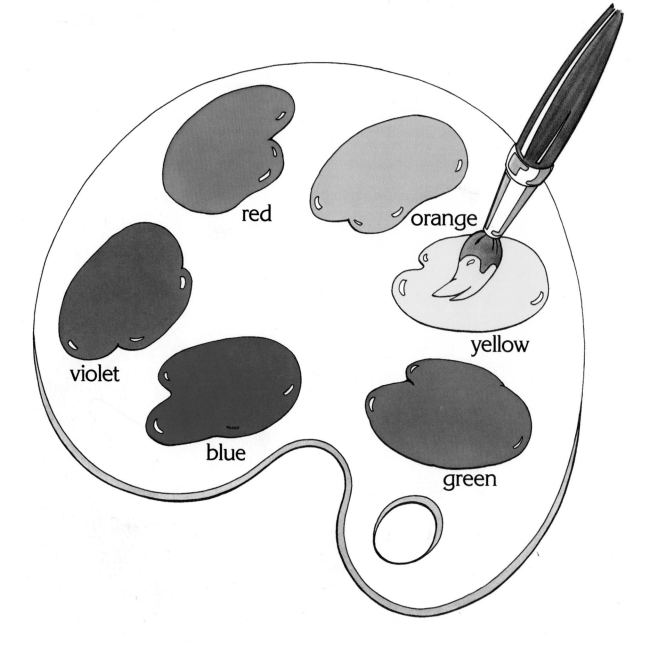

red

orange

violet

yellow

blue

green

This is a **color wheel**.

Can you name the colors?

What colors can you find?

8 Color Families

Looking and Thinking

Artists call these **families** of colors.

How are the colors in each family alike?

How are they different?

16

Claude Monet, St. Lazare Train Station, The Normandy Train, 1877, Oil on canvas, 1'11½" × 2'7". The Art Institute of Chicago, Collection of Mr. & Mrs. Martin Ryerson.

This was a train station in France.

Did the painter use one family of colors?

What might be some reasons?

 Warm and Cool Colors

Looking and Thinking

Georgia O'Keeffe, From the Plains II, 1954, Collection of Susan and David Workman. Reproduced with permission of the artist.

Artists call  **warm colors.**
What might be some reasons?

Ernest Lawson, Falls in Winter. *San Diego Museum of Art, Museum Purchase. (26-153)*

Artists call **cool colors**.

What might be some reasons?

10 Your Skin Can Tell You About Texture

Looking and Thinking

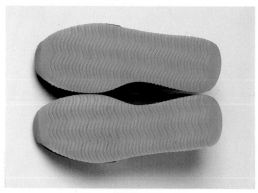

Texture can mean the way things feel.
Which texture do you want to feel first?
How do you know?

Can crayons teach your eyes about textures? How?

11 *Your Eyes Can Tell You About Texture*

Looking and Thinking

*Kurt Schwitters, Merz Konstruktion. Philadelphia
Museum of Art, A.E. Gallatin Collection.*

This collage is a group of textures.
Can your eyes tell you about textures? How?

Smooth and Rough

Making Art

Find textures from smooth to rough.
Use small paper to rub them.
Arrange the rubbings from smooth to rough.

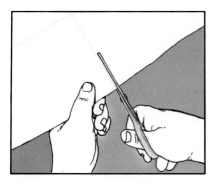

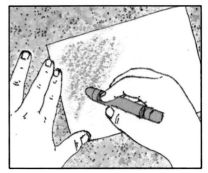

1. Cut.

2. Rub.

3. Rub.

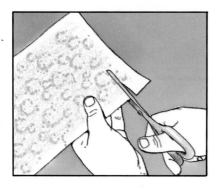

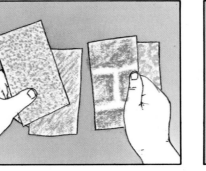

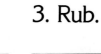

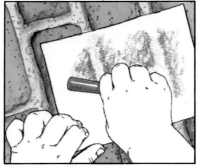

4. Trim.

5. Arrange.

6. Paste.

12 Remembering Textures

Looking and Thinking

What textures do you see in this picture?
How do you know about them?

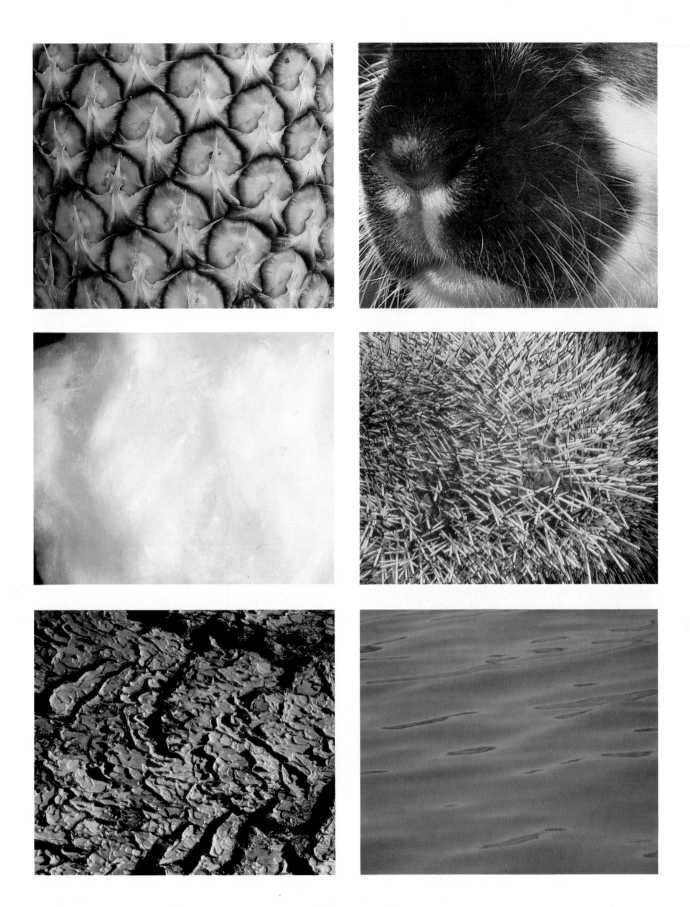

What do you think these textures are?

How do you know about them?

13 *Using Line, Shape, Color, and Texture*

Looking and Thinking

Eskimo, Mask, 19th Century, Wood, paint, feathers, leather, 45¼" x 21⅜" x 17⅞". The Metropolitan Museum of Art, The Michael C. Rockefeller Memorial Collection, Gift of Nelson A. Rockefeller, 1961. (1978.412.76)

Here are some new **masks** and an old mask.

How are they alike?

How are they different?

Making Art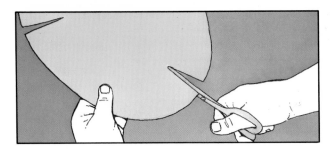

 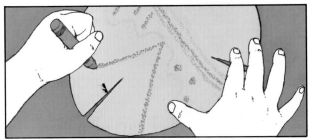

1. Cut top and bottom.

2. Add crayon or pen lines.

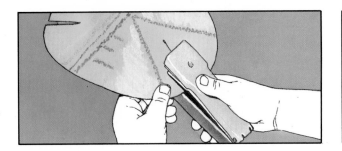 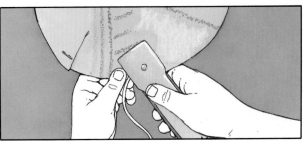

3. Overlap and staple.

4. Staple band.

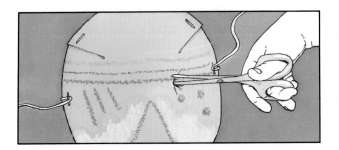 

5. Cut eye holes.

6. Make paper curls.

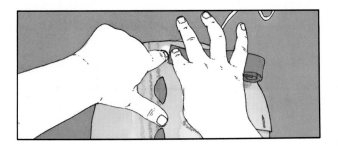 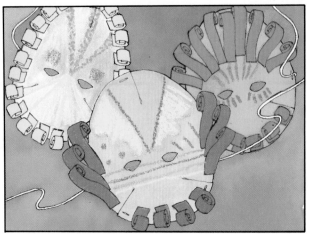

7. Paste curls on.

14 *Things in Front, Things Behind*

Looking and Thinking

Henri Rousseau, Jungle: Tiger Attacking a Buffalo, *1908, Oil on canvas, 67¾" × 75⅜". The Cleveland Museum of Art, Gift of the Hanna Fund.*

What things are close to you in this picture?

What things are farther away?

Making Art

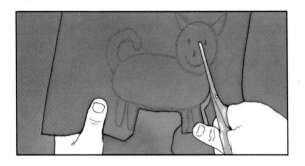

1. Cut out a cat.

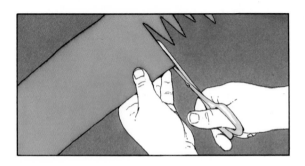

2. Cut out some plants.

3. Put the cat in the middle.

4. Paste them down.

15 *Circus Art*

Looking and Thinking

W.H. Brown, Bareback Riders, 1886, Cardboard, 18½" x 14½". National Gallery of Art, Smithsonian Institution, Washington, D.C., Gift of Edgar William and Bernice Chrysler Garbach.

What do you know about a circus?

Students made this mural.
What can you tell about it?

Exploring Art

Crafts

Anna Tuell, Marriage Quilt, 1785, Wadsworth Atheneum.

People like to make **crafts** by hand.
A mother made this quilt by hand.
Tell about other crafts you have seen.

Review

Looking at Art

Claude Monet, St. Lazare Train Station, The Normandy Train, 1877, Oil on canvas, 1'11½" x 2'7".
The Art Institute of Chicago, Collection of Mr. & Mrs. Martin Ryerson.

Look at the lines and shapes.
Look at the colors and textures.
What can you tell?

Unit 2

Looking More Closely

Grant Wood, Stone City, Iowa, 1930, *Oil on Wood. Collection, Joslyn Art Museum, Omaha, Nebraska.*

How are these two pictures alike?
How are they different?

16 Pictures of Scary Places

Looking and Thinking

Charles Burchfield, The Night Wind, *1918, Watercolor and gouache, 21½" x 27⅞". The Museum of Modern Art, New York, A. Gouget Goodyear Collection.*

What things does the painting tell about?

How does it make you feel?

How do these places make you feel?
Can you think of other scary places?

17 *Using a Paintbrush*

Looking and Thinking

Vincent van Gogh, *Sunflowers*, 1888, oil on canvas,
Neue Pinakothek, Munich.

An artist painted this picture.
How did he use his brush?

Making Art

Look what you can do!

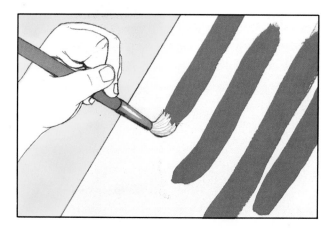

1. You can make thick lines.

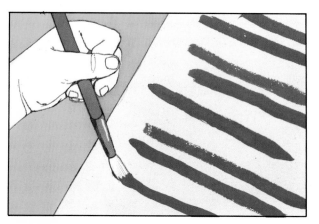

2. You can make thin lines.

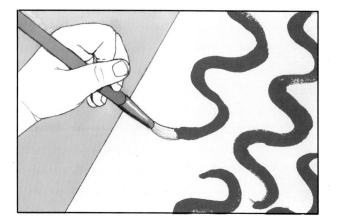

3. You can make curvy lines.

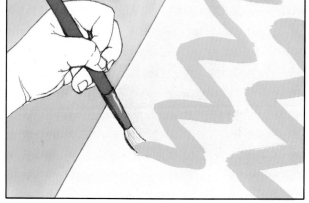

4. You can make zigzags.

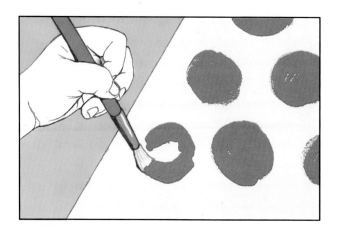

5. You can make big dots.

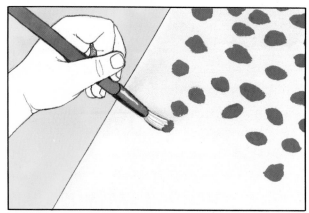

6. You can make small dots.

18 Mixing Colors

Looking and Thinking

Mix red and yellow. What do you get?

Mix yellow and blue. What do you get?

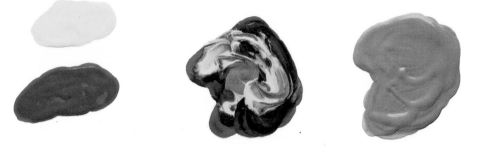

Mix blue and red. What do you get?

Making Art

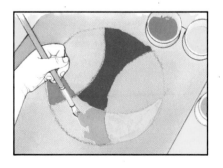

1. Draw around the plate.

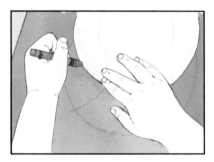

2. Make six spaces.

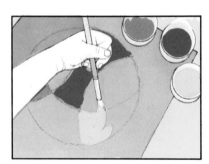

3. Paint red, yellow, and blue.

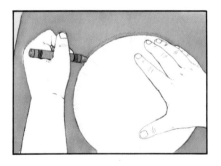

4. Mix orange and paint.

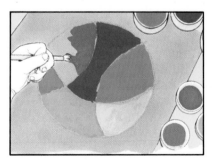

5. Paint green and violet.

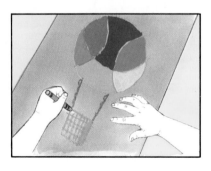

6. Make something round.

19 Light and Dark Colors

Looking and Thinking

Pablo Picasso, Le Gourmet, 1901, Canvas, 36½" × 26⅞". National Gallery of Art, Washington, Chester Dale Collection.

The artist chose blue for this picture.

Can you find dark blues?

Can you find light blues?

What makes colors light?

What makes colors dark?

1.

2.

3.

4.

5.

6.

7.

8.

What colors made these?

20 Patterns All Around You

Looking and Thinking

Papago basket, *Robert H. Lowie Museum of Anthropology, University of California, Berkeley, California.*

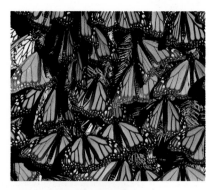

A **pattern** is something over and over.
Can you see patterns?
Can you find others?

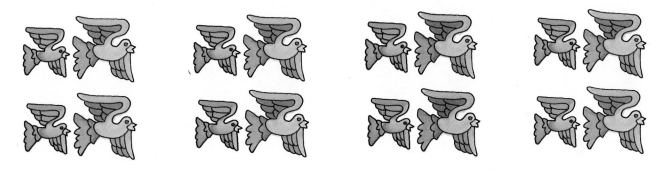

Can you clap to these patterns?

21 *What Comes Next in Patterns?*

Looking and Thinking

What comes next?

You can print a pattern.

22 *Over and Again in Patterns*

Looking and Thinking

Merry-Go-Round

I climbed up on the merry-go-round
And it went round and round.
I climbed up on a big brown horse
And it went up and down.

Around and round
And up and down,
Around and round
And up and down.
I sat high up
On a big brown horse
And rode around
On a merry-go-round

And rode around
On the merry-go-round
I rode around
On the merry-go-round
        Around
            And around
            And
                Round

Dorothy Baruch

What patterns can you find in the poem?

Does a  have patterns? What kind?

23 Lines, Shapes, and Patterns

Looking and Thinking

Vincent Van Gogh, Irises, 1889. The Joan Whitney Payson Collection, The Whitney Payson Gallery of Art, Westbrook College, Portland, Maine.

Look at each picture.

What lines do you see again and again?

What shapes do you see again and again?

Touch them.

Jesse Allen, Two Whales. Courtesy the Vorpal Galleries, New York City and San Francisco.

24 American Indians and Art

Looking and Thinking

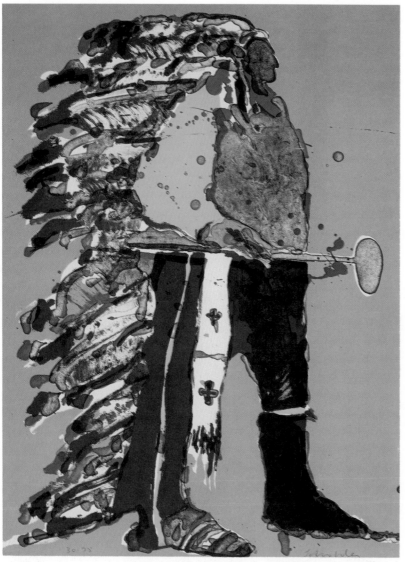

Fritz Scholder, American Indian with Tomahawk, 1975, Lithograph. Reproduced with permission of Fritz Scholder.

George Catlin, The White Cloud, Head Chief of the Iowas, c. 1845, Canvas, 27¾" × 22¾". National Gallery of Art, Washington, Paul Mellon Collection.

These artists tell a little about Indians.
How are the pictures alike?
How are they different?

What kinds of feathers have you seen?

What do these pictures tell about feathers?

Looking and Thinking

Can you find a fish behind another fish?
Can you find a fish in front of another fish?

 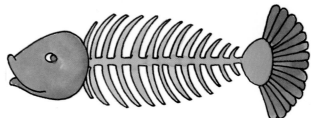

Patterns outside a fish   Patterns inside a fish

Making Art

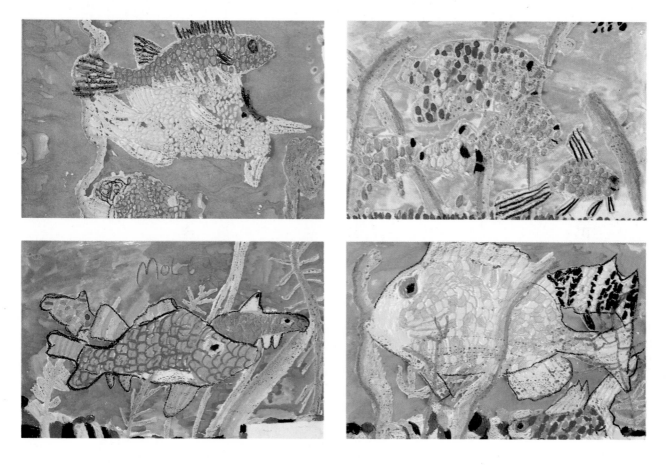

Draw some large fish.

Make some fish in front and some behind.

Draw some patterns on your fish.

26 *Decoration*

Looking and Thinking

Decorations are added to things.

How were decorations used in this picture?

Sometimes decorations say you belong.

Decorations make things nicer.

Decorations can make you smile.

27 *Decorating Things To Eat*

Looking and Thinking

Ecuadoran, Bread dolls, *from* Cookies and Bread, The Baker's Art, *by Ilse Johnson and N.S. Hazelton.*

What colors do you see?

What shapes do you see?

Is the food nice to look at? Why?

58

Making Art

You can decorate clay.

 *Weaving*

Looking and Thinking

This artist is **weaving**.
How does she do it?
Make some smart guesses.

Making Art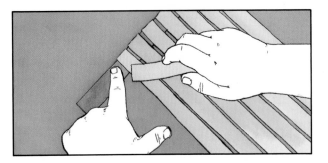

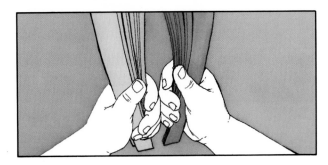

1. You need these strips.

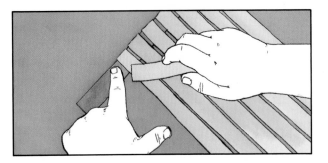

2. Paste on the dark ones.

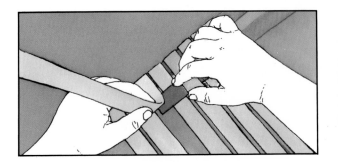

3. Go over under, over under.

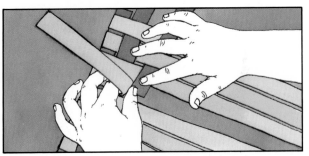

4. Go under over, under over.

5. Use all the strips.

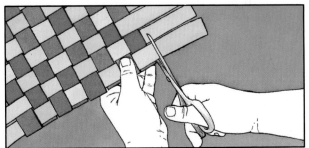

6. Paste and cut the ends.

29 Lines and Shapes in Letters

Looking and Thinking

Stuart Davis, Combination Concrete, 1958, Oil on canvas, 24¾" x 18⅛". Benenson Collection, Connecticut.

What is this picture about?

Did the artist use letters? Where?

A B C D E F G H I J K L M
N O P Q R S T U V W X Y Z

Which letters have straight lines?
Which letters have curved lines?
What shapes can you find?

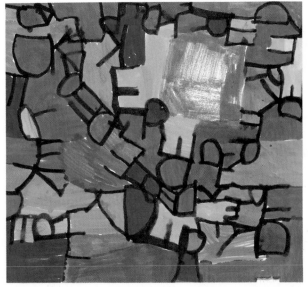

These are name pictures.

 **A Class
Book**

Looking and Thinking

Judy Graham
Michael Ansell

Bird's Eye

Cover art from Bird's Eye by Judy Graham, illustrated by Michael Ansell. Copyright © 1982 by The Green Tiger Press. Reproduced by permission of the publisher. All rights reserved.

Artists make pictures for books.
This picture is a book cover.

Donald Herberholz, Prints Charming. *Courtesy of the artist.*

One artist used fingerprints to make pictures.

You can make pictures this way.

You can make a class book.

Exploring Art

Picture Frames

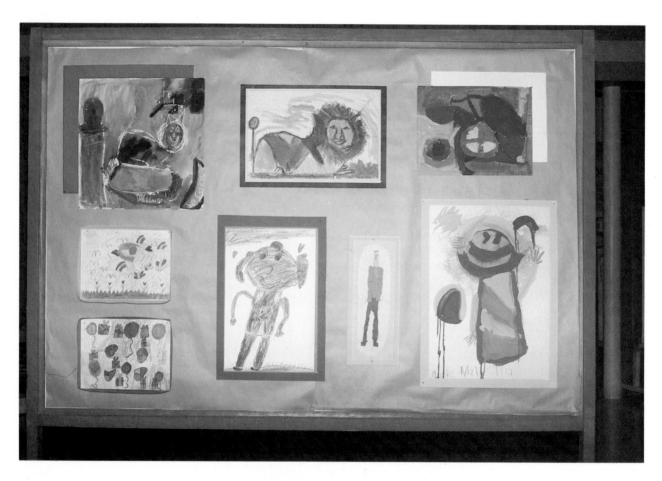

Frames make artwork look better.

Make some smart guesses about why.

Review

Creating Art

Pablo Picasso, Le Gourmet, 1901, Canvas, 36½" x 26⅞." National Gallery of Art, Washington, Chester Dale Collection.

What can you tell about this painting?

Think about these things.

Light and dark colors   pattern   decoration

Unit 3

How Artists See

Robert Vickrey, Flower Garden, *1961, Tempera/board 35¾" x 48". The San Diego Museum of Art Collection.*

Artists look closely.

They look at big things and at little things.

They look inside.

They look behind and under.

What do you think artists see?

Abastenia St. Leger Everle, Roller
Skating, *Before 1909, Bronze,*
13" x 11¾" x 6½." Collection of
the Whitney Museum of American Art.

31 *Artists Tell About Things in Their Own Ways*

Looking and Thinking

What do waves look like to you?
Can you guess? Do you know?

Bridget Riley, Current, *1964, Synthetic polymer paint on composition board, 58³⁄₈" x 58⁷⁄₈". Collection, The Museum of Modern Art, New York, Philip Johnson Fund.*

Katsushika Hokusai, The Great Wave, *from* Thirty-Six Views of Mt. Fuji, *Tokugawa period, early Nineteenth Century, print, 14³⁄₄" wide. Museum of Fine Arts, Boston.*

Two artists told about waves in these pictures.

What do they tell you?

32 *Some Artists and Their Work*

Looking and Thinking

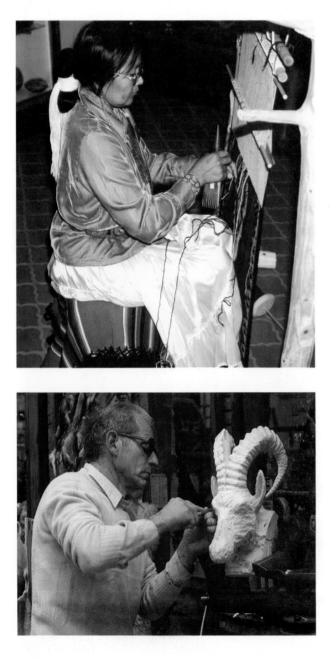

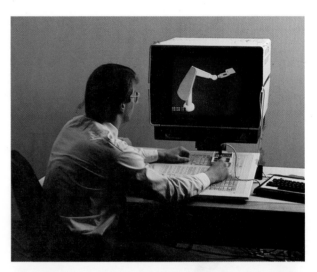

What are these artists doing?

What are they making?

One artist works this way.
Make some smart guesses
  about why.

Making Art

1. Make seven
   shapes.

2. You choose.

3. Fill in with lines.

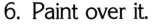

4. Make yours
   different.

5. Make wavy lines.

6. Paint over it.

33 Artists Paint Places

Looking and Thinking

Claude Monet, Rue Saint Denis, Fete du 30 Juin 1878, *Musee des Beaux-Arts, Giraudon/Art Resource, NY.*

Artists paint pictures of places they like.

They paint **views** they like.

74

Lyonel Feninger, Sailboats, 1929, oil on canvas, 17" × 28½". The Detroit Institute of Arts, Gift of Robert H. Tannahill.

What views did these artists like?

What do they tell you?

He found a view he likes.

Now he will make a picture of the view.

Looking and Thinking

Vincent van Gogh, La Mousme, 1888, Canvas, 28⅞" × 23¾". National Gallery of Art, Washington, Chester Dale Collection.

Artists paint pictures of people.
What does the artist say about this person?

Mary Cassat, Children Playing on the Beach, 1884, Oil on canvas, 38⅜" × 29¼". National Gallery of Art, Washington, Ailsa Mellon Bruce Collection.

What did the artist see?

What do you think she felt?

35 *Artists Paint What They Like*

Looking and Thinking

Margaretta Angelica Peale, Still Life with Watermelon and Peaches, 1828, Oil on canvas, 13" × 19⅛". Smith College Museum of Art, Northampton, Massachusetts.

What did this artist like?

What colors did she use?

Wayne Thiebaud, Pie Counter, 1963, Oil, 30" × 36". Collection of Whitney Museum of American Art, Larry Aldrich Foundation Fund. Acq. #64.11

This artist liked rows of pies.

What shapes can you find?

36 Artists and Animals

Looking and Thinking

Do you like to look at animals?
Do you like to touch cat's fur?

Ch'ing Dynasty, 18th century. Spring Play in a T'ang Garden, Handscroll, colors on silk, 14¾" × 104". The Metropolitan Museum of Art, Fletcher Fund, 1947.

Egypt, The Gayer-Anderson Bastet Cat, after 30 BC, Bronze. The British Museum, Presented by R. G. Gayer-Anderson and Mary Stout.

What did these artists tell about cats?

Making Art

1. Wet paper with clear water.

2. Blot with newspaper.

3. Paint two ovals. Let dry.

4. Add some lines.

5. You decide.

6. Make yours different.

37 *We Live with Art*

Looking and Thinking

These things were all made to be used.

They were made to look nice too.

Some artists planned these things.
Artists make things to use that look nice.
What other things do you think artists make?

38 Lines Tell About Texture

Looking and Thinking

What lines do you see in these pictures?

What do the lines help you know?

Rembrandt van Rijn, Study of an Elephant, *1637, Black chalk, 7" x 10". The Albertina Collection, Hofburg Esperanto Museum, Vienna, Austria.*

Look at the lines in this picture.
What do the lines tell about the elephant?

Texture is how something feels.
Do the lines help tell about texture?

39 *Shapes in Nature*

Looking and Thinking

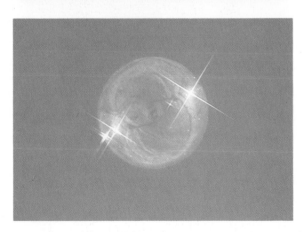

What can you tell about these shapes?

People use shapes from nature in many ways.

Student artists used ★ ★ ★ ★ ★
They even made wishes!

40 *Forms Take Up Space*

Looking and Thinking

You have a front, sides, and a back.
You take up **space**.
Forms take up space.

What can you tell about these forms?

How are they like shapes?

How are they different?

41 Sculpture Has a Front, Sides, and a Back

Looking and Thinking

Eduardo Paolozzi, Japanese War God, 1958, Bronze, 64½" × 13" × 22". Albright-Knox Art Gallery, Buffalo, New York, Gift of Seymour H. Knox, 1960.

Pablo Picasso, Baboon and Young, 1951, Bronze (cast 1955), after found objects, 21" high, base 13¼" × 6⅞". Collection, The Museum of Modern Art, New York, Mrs. Simon Guggenheim Fund.

You can walk around **sculpture**.

You can look at shapes, lines, and spaces.

Have you built a sculpture like this?

Making Art

You can be a **sculptor**.
You can make something different.

1. Fold and paint.

2. Cut and staple.

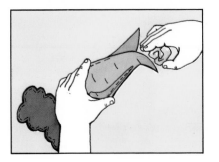

3. Fill with paper.

4. Staple end.

42 *Sculptures of People*

Looking and Thinking

Teotihuacan, Mexico, Reclining Man with Shaved Head, *400-900, Ceramic, 4¾". Museo Nacional de Antropologia.*

Henry Moore, Draped Reclining Figure (rear view), *1952-53, Bronze. Hirshhorn Museum and Sculpture Garden, Smithsonian Institution.*

What can you tell about these sculptures?

Making Art

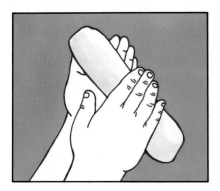

1. Make a log.

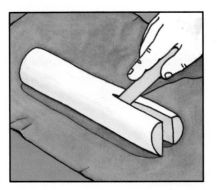

2. Cut two legs.

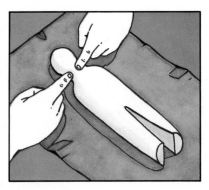

3. Make a neck and a head.

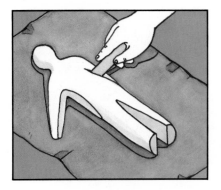

4. Make arms like this.

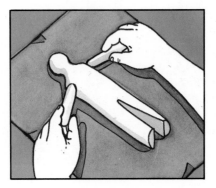

5. Or add on arms.

6. Make two feet.

43 *A Puppet for Your Pencil*

Looking and Thinking

These are **puppets**.

But sometimes you might forget!

Making Art

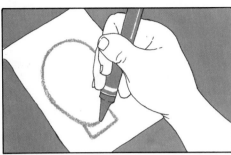

1. Draw an egg shape.

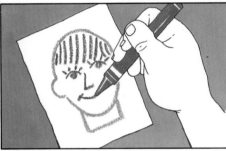

2. Draw a face.

3. Cut it out.

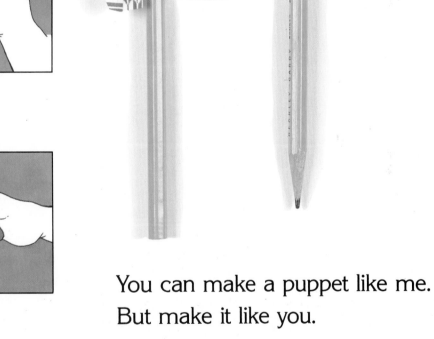

You can make a puppet like me.
But make it like you.

4. Make some clothes.

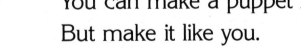

5. Tape it.

44 *A Puppet for Your Finger*

Looking and Thinking

Paul Klee, Modern Magic puppets, created for his son, Felix: Eskimo, and Scarecrow. *Reprinted by permission from* The Art of the Puppet, *by Bil Baird. Publishers: Plays-Inc., Boston, MA.*

This artist made puppets for his son.
Puppets can say anything you want them to.
Do you know why?

Making Art

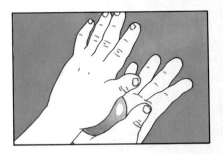

1. Roll a ball.

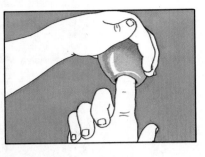

2. Push it on.

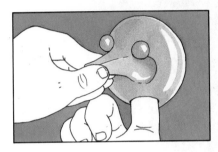

3. Make a nose, mouth, and eyes.

4. Make a mouth and ears.

5. Can you make hair?

6. Paint your puppet.

7. Add more colors.

8. Dress it up.

45 *Having a Puppet Show*

Looking and Thinking

Puppet plays can look like this.
What do you think they are saying?

Think about a problem.
Think about an end.
Make your puppet move and talk.

Exploring Art

Art Careers

Artists can have many kinds of **careers**.
This artist is a **designer**.
Can you think of other art careers?

Review

Knowing About Art

Henry Moore, Draped Reclining Figure (rear view), 1952-53, Bronze. Hirshhorn Museum and Sculpture Garden, Smithsonian Institution.

What kinds of art do artists make?
What do they show in their art?
What other things do artists do?

Unit 4

Thinking Like an Artist

Winslow Homer, The Country School, 1871, Oil on canvas, 21³/₈" x 38³/₈." The Saint Louis Art Museum, Museum Purchase.

Andre Derain, The Old Bridge, 1910, Canvas, 37⅞" x 39½." National Gallery of Art, Washington, Chester Dale Collection.

Artists like to think in new ways.

They get to play with ideas.

What were these artists thinking?

Make some smart guesses.

46 *Looking at Old Things in New Ways*

Looking and Thinking

What do you think this is?

The artist wanted you to see it with new eyes.

What ways did the artist help you?

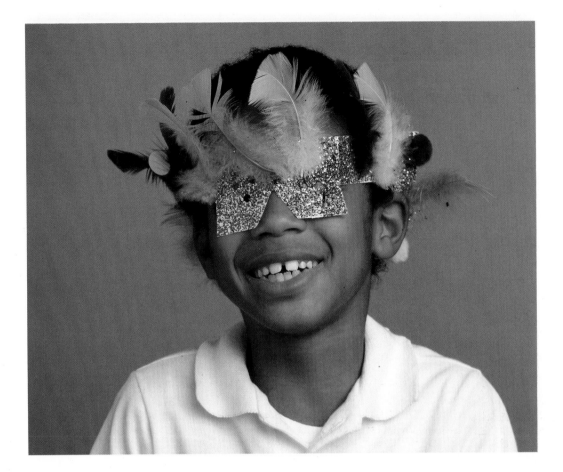

These magic glasses help you see in new ways.

Making Art 🔷

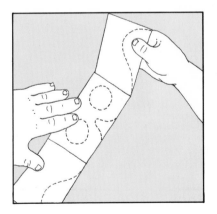

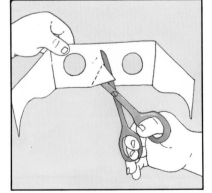

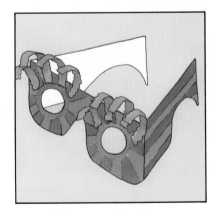

1. Fold.

2. Cut.

3. Decorate.

47 **Thinking Like Artists**

Looking and Thinking

Artists use old things in new ways.

Alexander Calder, Chock, 1972, Metal, 11" x 28" x 22". Collection of Whitney Museum of American Art, Gift of the artist. Acq.#72.55

What things did the artist use?
Make some smart guesses about why.

106

Look at this picture.

But first put on your magic glasses.

How might you use these things?

48 Artists Tell About Our World

Looking and Thinking

Thomas Eakins, Baby at Play, [18]76, Oil on canvas, 32¼" × 48⅜". National Gallery of Art, Washington, John Hay Whitney Collection.

How did this artist use shape and texture?

What does he tell you?

Mary Cassatt, The Boating Party, *1893/1894, Canvas, 35½" × 46⅛". National Gallery of Art, Washington, Chester Dale Collection.*

How did this artist use color and lines?

What does she tell you?

49 Pictures for Poems About Weather

Looking and Thinking

Hello and Good-bye

Hello and good-bye
Hello and good-bye

When I'm in a swing
Swinging low and then high
Goodbye to the ground
Hello to the sky.

Hello to the rain
Goodbye to the sun,
Then hello again sun
When the rain is all done.

In blows the winter,
Away the birds fly.
Goodbye and hello
Hello and good-bye.

Mary Ann Hoberman

Students read "Hello and Good-bye."
Then they made these pictures.

Read this with your teacher.
What will you tell in your picture?

Understanding

Sun

and rain

and wind

and storms

and thunder go together.

There has to be a little bit of each

to make the

weather.

Myra Cohn Livingston

50 Architects Plan Beautiful Buildings

Looking and Thinking

An **architect** is an artist who plans buildings.

Which building do you like best? Why?
Use the word *shape* in one reason.

You can build a beautiful city of tall buildings.

Making Art

1. Fold.

2. Fold again.

3. Cut.

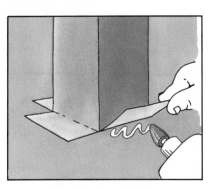

4. Bend.

5. Glue in place.

6. Draw streets.

51 Architects Plan Places to Live

Looking and Thinking

These are places to live.
How are they alike?
Where would you like to live?

A House is a House for Me

A hill is a house for an ant, an ant.
A hive is a house for a bee.
A hole is a house for a mole or a mouse
And a house is a house for me!

A web is a house for a spider.
A bird builds its nest in a tree.
There is nothing so snug as a bug in a rug
And a house is a house for me!

Mary Ann Hoberman

What would be just the house for you?
Plan one for yourself.

52 Places and Spaces to Play

Looking and Thinking

Think of places and spaces where you like to play.

Think up some new ones.

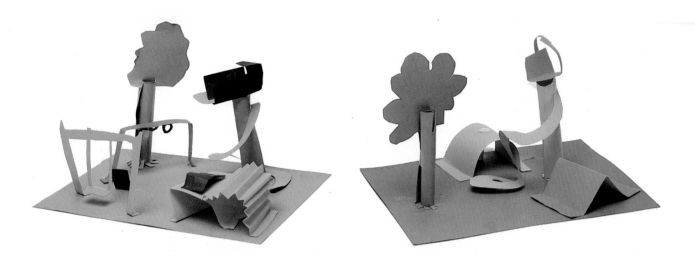

Student artists made these play spaces.

Making Art 🔶 THINK SAFETY

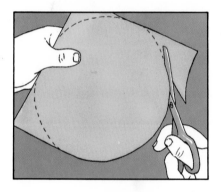

1. Cut off corners.

2. Cut a path.

3. Roll some paper.

53 Textures and Patterns in Cloth

Looking and Thinking

Look at the pictures of cloth.

What patterns can you find?

How would you tell about the textures?

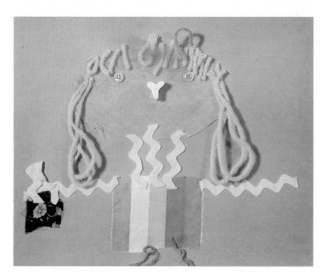

Students made cloth collages.
Choose one for your bedroom.
Why did you choose it?

54 *Imagination and Patterns*

Looking and Thinking

Jasper Johns, Three Flags, 1958, Encaustic on canvas, 30⅞" x 45½" x 5." Collection of the Whitney Museum of American Art, 50th Anniversary gift of the Gilman Foundation, Inc., the Lauder Foundation, A. Alfred Taubman, an anonymous doner (and purchase). Acq. #80.32

What do you see in the picture?
Which shapes make patterns?

Artists made the cloth.
Artists made the clothes.
What patterns can you find?

55 *Circle Patterns, Circle Art*

Looking and Thinking

Find some colors used over and over.
Where are some patterns of lines?

Look at the circles.

What can you find over and over?

Students made this art.

What patterns can you find?

56 Eggs: Alike and Different

Looking and Thinking

Look at all the eggs.

What patterns can you find?

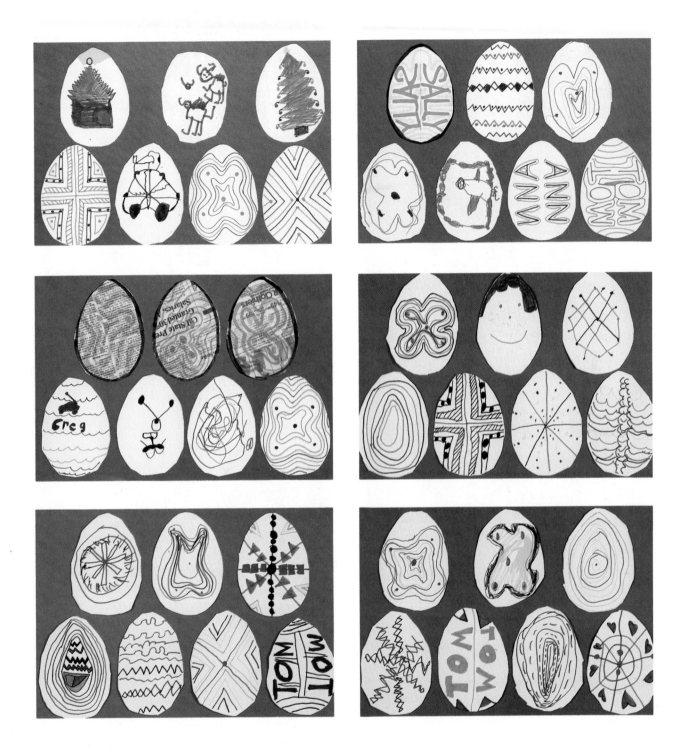

Students made these eggs.
Can you find any eggs with the same pattern?

57 Artists Can Make What They Want

Looking and Thinking

Being an artist can be fun.
You can make what you want.
What did these artists want?

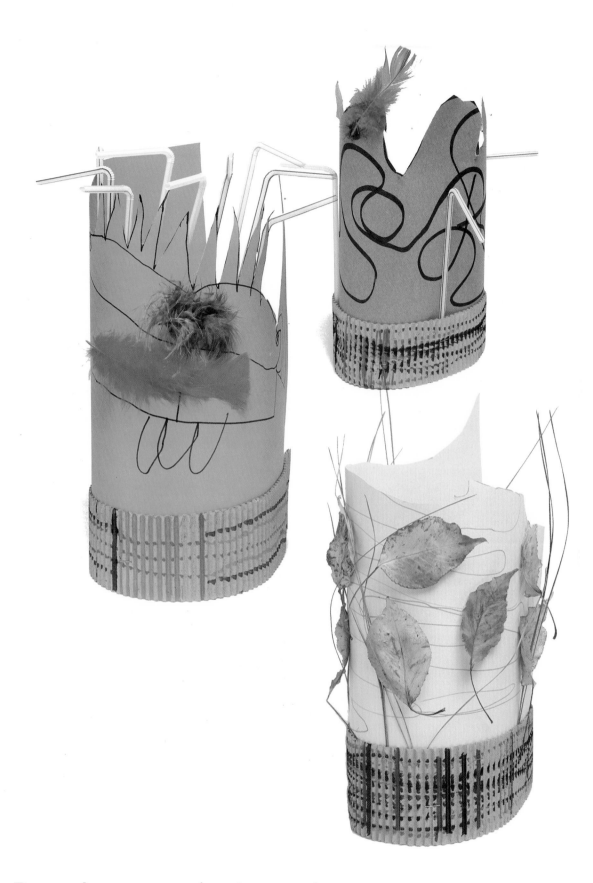

Pretend you are going to a party.
And you need a hat.
What will you make?

58 Artists Use Paint in Different Ways

Looking and Thinking

Pierre Auguste Renoir, The Luncheon of the Boating Party, *1881, Oil on canvas, 51"× 68". The Phillips Collection, Washington. D.C.*

Look at the two paintings.

What differences do you see?

Sam Francis, Towards Disappearance, II, 1958, Oil on canvas, 9' ½" x 10' 5⅞." Collection, The Museum of Modern Art, New York, Blanchette Rockefeller Fund.

Making Art

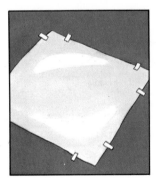   

1. Tape it down.

2. Use a little paint.

3. Make shapes and textures.

4. Rub paper gently.

129

59 Spatters, Dabs, and Blots

Looking and Thinking

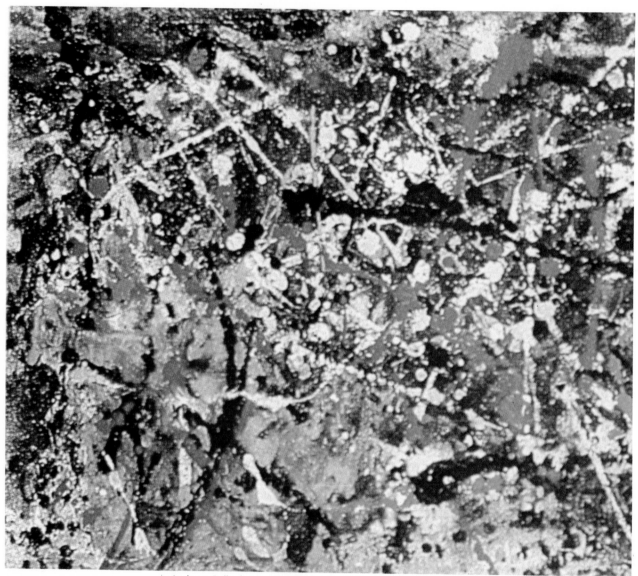

Jackson Pollock, Number 25 (detail), 1950. Hirshhorn Museum and Sculpture Garden, Smithsonian Institution, Washington, D.C.

This is part of a long painting.
The artist liked to dribble and spatter.
What can you tell about it?

Making Art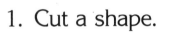

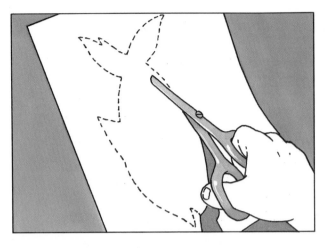

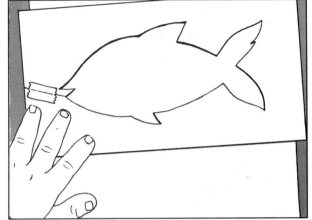

1. Cut a shape.

2. Put it on paper.

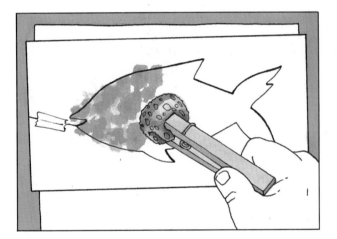

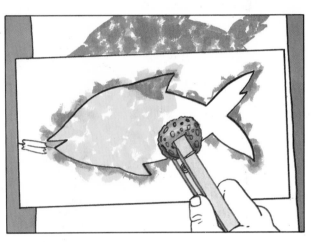

3. Dab it with paint.

4. Move it.

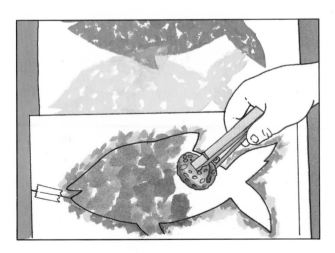

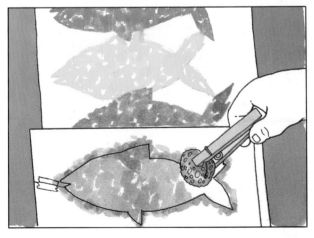

5. Use another color.

6. Use another.

60 *Having an Art Show*

Looking and Thinking

Artists like to show their work.

They choose their best art.

Choose your best art work.
Have a class art show.

Exploring Art

Summer Art

What artwork will you create this summer?
Work with your class.
List as many ideas as you can.

Review

Making Up Your Mind About Art

Wassily Kandinsky, Russian, 1866-1944, Improvisation 31 (Sea Battle), *1913, Canvas, 55⅜" x 47⅛". National Gallery of Art, Washington, Ailsa Mellon Bruce Fund.*

Do you like this painting? Why?
Would you want it in your room? Why?
Find a picture you like better. Tell why.

Acknowledgments

We gratefully acknowledge the valuable contributions of the following artists, consultants, editorial advisors, and reviewers who participated in the development of this book: Ruth Jones and C.J. Greenwald, teachers, St. Luke's Lutheran Day School, La Mesa, CA; Mirta Golino, art educator and editorial advisor, San Diego; Jeff Jurich, animator and writer, Celluloid Studios, Denver; Dennis Smith, sculptor, Highland, UT; Virginia Gadzala, costume designer, San Diego; Phyllis Thurston, former Art Supervisor, Pinellas County School District, Clearwater, FL; Judy Chicago and Mary Ross Taylor, Through the Flower, Benicia, CA; Andrew Blanks, Jr., art teacher, Johnston Middle School, Houston; Barbara Pearson Roberts, teacher, Sabal Palm Elementary School, Tallahassee; Shirley and Terry McManus, puppetry consultants, "Puppets Please," San Diego; Dr. Wayne Woodward, associate professor of art education, Georgia Southwestern College; Mary Riggs of Riggs Galleries, San Diego; Anna Ganahl, Director of Public Relations, Art Center College of Design, Pasadena; Françoise Gilot, artist, La Jolla, CA; Leven C. Leatherbury, independent consultant in art education, San Diego; Betty Cavanaugh, curriculum consultant in art education, Upland, CA; Joel Hagen, artist and writer, Oakdale, CA; Kellene Champlin, Art Supervisor, Fulton County Schools, Atlanta; Mar Gwen Land, art teacher, Montgomery Jr. High School, San Diego; LaRene McGregor, fiber artist, McKenzie Bridge, OR; Norma Wilson, former art teacher and editorial advisor, San Diego; Dr. Ann S. Richardson, Supervisor of Art, Foreign Languages, and Gifted and Talented Education, Charles County Public Schools, La Plata, MD; Talli Larrick, educator and writer, El Cajon, California; Mary Apuli, Coordinator of Elementary Program, Indiana School District No. 16, Minneapolis; Carol Widdop-Sonka, artist and writer, San Diego; Virginia Fitzpatrick, art educator and writer, Bloomington, IN; Evelyn Ackerman, artist, Era Industries, Culver City, CA; Judy Kugel, teacher trainer for Learning to Read Through the Arts, New York City; Arlie Zolynas, educator and author, San Diego; Nancy Remington, Principal, Sacramento County Day School, Sacramento; Kay Alexander, Art Consultant, Palo Alto School District, Palo Alto, CA; Billie Phillips, Lead Art Supervisor, St. Louis Public Schools, St. Louis; Sister Marie Albert, S.S.J., Principal, St. Callistus School, Philadelphia; Robert Vickrey, artist, Orleans, MA.

We especially appreciate the students from the following schools who contributed the student art reproduced in this series: O.H. Anderson Elem. School, Mahtomedi, MN; Atkinson Elem. School, Barnesville, MN; W.D. Hall Elem. School, El Cajon, CA; Idlewild Elem. School, Memphis, TN; Irving Elem. School, St. Louis, MO; MacArthur Elem. School, Indianapolis, IN; Oakwood Elem. School, Knoxville, TN; John Roe Elem. School, St. Louis, MO; Taylors Falls School District #140, Taylors Falls, MN; Washington Elem. School, Pomona, CA; Enterprise Elem. School, Enterprise, FL; Kellogg Elem. School, Chula Vista, CA; Learning to Read Through the Arts, New York, NY; Lewis School, San Diego, CA; Woodcrest Elem. School, Fridley, MN; Westwood Elem. School, San Diego, CA; Independent School District #16, Minneapolis, MN; St. Luke's Lutheran Day School, La Mesa, CA; Country Day School, Sacramento, CA; Budd School, Fairmont, MN; Park Terrace Elem. School, Spring Lake Park, MN; Audubon Elem. School, Baton Rouge, LA; Chilowee Elem. School, Knoxville, TN; Logan Elem. School, San Diego, CA; Grassy Creek Elem. School, Indianapolis, IN; Earle Brown Elem. School, Brooklyn Center, MN; Jefferson Elem. School, Winona, MN; Calvert Elem. School, Prince Frederick, MD; Barnsville Elem. School, Barnsville, MN; Ridgedale Elem. School, Knoxville, TN; Children's Creative and Performing Arts Academy, San Diego, CA; Steven V. Correia School, San Diego, CA; Walnut Park Elem. School, St. Louis, MO.

Although it is impossible to acknowledge all the contributors to this project, we express special thanks for the generous efforts of the following individuals: Janet Reim, Gail Kozar, Rae Murphy, Jan Thompson, Gerald Williams, Timothy Asfazadour, Judy Cannon, Helen Negley, Crystal Thorson, Rachelle and Tyler Bruford, Mary Bluhm, David Zielinski, David Oliver, Daniel and Carl Bohman, Anne G. Allen, Bao Vuong, Gail W. Guth, Signe Ringbloom, Claire Murphy, Joan Blaine, Patrice M. Sparks, and Larke Johnston.

Coronado Staff: Marsha Barrett Lippincott, Level One Editor; Janet Kylstad Coulon, Level Two Editor; Deanne Kells Cordell, Level Three Editor; Carol Spirkoff Prime, Level Four Editor; Patricia McCambridge, Level Five Editor; DeLynn Decker, Level Six Editor; Janis Heppell, Project Designer; Lisa Peters, Designer; Myrtali Anagnostopoulos, Designer; Debra Saleny, Photo Research.